Sweet Treats: 50 Desserts for Every Occasion

By: Kelly Johnson

Table of Contents

- Classic Tiramisu
- Chocolate Lava Cake
- Lemon Meringue Pie
- Vanilla Bean Panna Cotta
- Red Velvet Cupcakes
- Apple Crumble
- Cheesecake with Berry Compote
- Chocolate Chip Cookies
- Strawberry Shortcake
- Raspberry Sorbet
- Coconut Macaroons
- Carrot Cake with Cream Cheese Frosting
- Profiteroles with Chocolate Sauce
- Crème Brûlée
- Peach Cobbler
- Key Lime Pie
- Baklava
- Pavlova with Fresh Fruit
- S'mores Bars
- Churros with Cinnamon Sugar
- Blueberry Muffins
- Chocolate Eclairs
- Almond Joy Brownies
- Classic Banana Pudding
- Fruit Tart with Pastry Cream
- Sticky Toffee Pudding
- Lemon Bars
- Pistachio Gelato
- Chocolate Truffles
- Coconut Cream Pie
- Apple Fritters
- Baked Alaska
- Chocolate-Dipped Strawberries
- Cinnamon Rolls with Icing
- Molten Chocolate Mug Cake

- Pear and Almond Galette
- Salted Caramel Flan
- Tarte Tatin
- Pumpkin Pie
- Chocolate Pots de Crème
- Butterscotch Pudding
- Orange Sorbet
- Snickerdoodle Cookies
- Chocolate-Covered Pretzels
- Mousse au Chocolat
- Fruit and Cream Parfaits
- Ricotta Cheesecake
- Almond Cake with Apricot Glaze
- Lavender Honey Ice Cream
- Zucchini Bread with Walnuts

Classic Tiramisu

Ingredients:

- 6 large egg yolks
- 3/4 cup granulated sugar
- 1 1/2 cups mascarpone cheese
- 1 1/2 cups heavy cream
- 2 cups brewed coffee, cooled
- 2 tbsp dark rum or coffee liqueur (optional)
- 2 packs ladyfingers
- Unsweetened cocoa powder for dusting
- Dark chocolate shavings (optional)

Instructions:

1. In a heatproof bowl, whisk the egg yolks and sugar together over simmering water until pale and thick.
2. Add the mascarpone cheese to the yolk mixture, stirring until smooth.
3. In a separate bowl, whip the heavy cream until stiff peaks form, then fold it into the mascarpone mixture.
4. Combine the coffee and rum (if using) in a shallow dish. Quickly dip each ladyfinger into the coffee mixture, then layer them in a serving dish.
5. Spread half of the mascarpone mixture over the soaked ladyfingers. Repeat with another layer of dipped ladyfingers and the remaining mascarpone mixture.
6. Cover and refrigerate for at least 4 hours, or overnight.
7. Dust with cocoa powder and garnish with chocolate shavings before serving.

Chocolate Lava Cake

Ingredients:

- 1/2 cup unsalted butter
- 6 oz semisweet chocolate, chopped
- 1/2 cup powdered sugar
- 2 large eggs
- 2 large egg yolks
- 1/4 cup all-purpose flour
- 1/4 tsp salt
- Vanilla ice cream for serving (optional)

Instructions:

1. Preheat the oven to 425°F (220°C). Grease and flour four ramekins.
2. In a microwave-safe bowl, melt the butter and chocolate together in 30-second intervals, stirring in between, until smooth.
3. Stir in the powdered sugar, then add the eggs and egg yolks, mixing until well combined.
4. Gently fold in the flour and salt.
5. Divide the batter evenly among the prepared ramekins.
6. Bake for 12-14 minutes until the edges are set but the center is soft.
7. Let the cakes sit for 1 minute before carefully inverting them onto plates. Serve warm with vanilla ice cream.

Lemon Meringue Pie

Ingredients:

For the crust:

- 1 1/4 cups all-purpose flour
- 1/4 cup powdered sugar
- 1/2 tsp salt
- 1/2 cup unsalted butter, cold and cubed
- 2-3 tbsp ice water

For the filling:

- 1 1/2 cups granulated sugar
- 1/4 cup cornstarch
- 1/4 tsp salt
- 1 1/2 cups water
- 4 large egg yolks, lightly beaten
- 1/2 cup fresh lemon juice
- 1 tbsp lemon zest
- 2 tbsp unsalted butter

For the meringue:

- 4 large egg whites
- 1/2 tsp cream of tartar
- 1/4 cup granulated sugar

Instructions:

1. Preheat the oven to 375°F (190°C). In a food processor, combine the flour, powdered sugar, and salt. Add the cold butter and pulse until the mixture resembles crumbs.
2. Gradually add ice water, pulsing until a dough forms. Press into a pie dish and bake for 15 minutes.
3. For the filling, whisk together sugar, cornstarch, and salt in a saucepan. Add water and bring to a boil, whisking constantly.
4. Gradually whisk in the egg yolks, lemon juice, and zest. Return to the heat and cook until thickened, about 2 minutes. Remove from heat and stir in butter.

5. For the meringue, beat the egg whites and cream of tartar until soft peaks form. Gradually add sugar and continue to beat until stiff peaks form.
6. Pour the lemon filling into the pie crust and top with meringue. Bake for 10-12 minutes, or until the meringue is golden.
7. Cool before serving.

Vanilla Bean Panna Cotta

Ingredients:

- 1 1/2 cups heavy cream
- 1 1/2 cups whole milk
- 1/2 cup granulated sugar
- 1 vanilla bean, split and scraped (or 1 tbsp vanilla extract)
- 2 1/4 tsp unflavored gelatin
- 3 tbsp water

Instructions:

1. In a saucepan, combine heavy cream, milk, and sugar. Heat over medium heat until the sugar dissolves.
2. Add the vanilla bean seeds and pod (or vanilla extract) and bring to a simmer.
3. In a separate small bowl, sprinkle gelatin over water and let it bloom for 5 minutes.
4. Remove the cream mixture from the heat and stir in the bloomed gelatin until dissolved.
5. Strain the mixture through a fine sieve and pour into serving glasses or molds.
6. Chill in the refrigerator for at least 4 hours, or until set.
7. Serve with fresh berries or fruit compote.

Red Velvet Cupcakes

Ingredients:

- 1 1/2 cups all-purpose flour
- 1 cup granulated sugar
- 1 tsp cocoa powder
- 1/2 tsp baking powder
- 1/4 tsp baking soda
- 1/4 tsp salt
- 1/2 cup vegetable oil
- 1 large egg
- 1 tsp vanilla extract
- 1/2 cup buttermilk
- 1 tbsp red food coloring
- 1/2 tsp white vinegar

For the frosting:

- 8 oz cream cheese, softened
- 1/4 cup unsalted butter, softened
- 2 cups powdered sugar
- 1 tsp vanilla extract

Instructions:

1. Preheat the oven to 350°F (175°C) and line a muffin tin with cupcake liners.
2. In a bowl, whisk together flour, sugar, cocoa powder, baking powder, baking soda, and salt.
3. In another bowl, whisk together oil, egg, vanilla extract, buttermilk, red food coloring, and vinegar.
4. Gradually add the wet ingredients to the dry ingredients, mixing until smooth.
5. Divide the batter among the cupcake liners and bake for 18-20 minutes, or until a toothpick comes out clean.
6. For the frosting, beat together cream cheese and butter until smooth. Gradually add powdered sugar and vanilla, mixing until fluffy.
7. Frost the cooled cupcakes and enjoy!

Apple Crumble

Ingredients:

For the filling:

- 4 cups apples, peeled and sliced
- 1/2 cup granulated sugar
- 1 tbsp lemon juice
- 1 tsp cinnamon
- 1/4 tsp nutmeg
- 1 tbsp cornstarch

For the topping:

- 3/4 cup all-purpose flour
- 1/2 cup rolled oats
- 1/2 cup brown sugar
- 1/2 cup unsalted butter, cold and cubed
- 1/4 tsp salt

Instructions:

1. Preheat the oven to 350°F (175°C). In a bowl, combine apples, sugar, lemon juice, cinnamon, nutmeg, and cornstarch. Toss to coat and transfer to a baking dish.
2. For the topping, combine flour, oats, brown sugar, and salt. Add the cold butter and rub it in with your fingers until the mixture resembles crumbs.
3. Sprinkle the topping evenly over the apple mixture.
4. Bake for 35-40 minutes, or until the apples are tender and the topping is golden brown.
5. Serve warm with vanilla ice cream or whipped cream.

Cheesecake with Berry Compote

Ingredients:

For the crust:

- 1 1/2 cups graham cracker crumbs
- 1/4 cup granulated sugar
- 1/2 cup unsalted butter, melted

For the filling:

- 3 (8 oz) packages cream cheese, softened
- 1 cup granulated sugar
- 3 large eggs
- 1 tsp vanilla extract
- 1/4 cup sour cream

For the berry compote:

- 2 cups mixed berries (strawberries, blueberries, raspberries)
- 1/4 cup sugar
- 1 tbsp lemon juice

Instructions:

1. Preheat the oven to 325°F (165°C). In a bowl, combine graham cracker crumbs, sugar, and melted butter. Press into the bottom of a springform pan.
2. For the filling, beat the cream cheese and sugar until smooth. Add eggs one at a time, mixing well after each addition. Stir in vanilla and sour cream.
3. Pour the filling over the crust and bake for 50-60 minutes, or until the center is set.
4. For the compote, combine the berries, sugar, and lemon juice in a saucepan. Cook over medium heat until the berries break down and the mixture thickens, about 10 minutes.
5. Let the cheesecake cool before topping with the berry compote.

Chocolate Chip Cookies

Ingredients:

- 2 1/4 cups all-purpose flour
- 1/2 tsp baking soda
- 1 cup unsalted butter, softened
- 3/4 cup granulated sugar
- 3/4 cup packed brown sugar
- 1 tsp vanilla extract
- 2 large eggs
- 2 cups semisweet chocolate chips
- 1/2 tsp salt

Instructions:

1. Preheat the oven to 350°F (175°C). Line baking sheets with parchment paper.
2. In a bowl, whisk together flour and baking soda. Set aside.
3. In a large bowl, cream together butter, granulated sugar, brown sugar, and vanilla extract until fluffy.
4. Add the eggs one at a time, mixing well after each.
5. Gradually add the dry ingredients and mix until combined. Stir in the chocolate chips.
6. Drop rounded tablespoons of dough onto the prepared baking sheets.
7. Bake for 10-12 minutes, or until golden brown. Let cool on a wire rack.

Strawberry Shortcake

Ingredients:

For the shortcake:

- 2 cups all-purpose flour
- 1/4 cup granulated sugar
- 1 tbsp baking powder
- 1/2 tsp salt
- 1/2 cup unsalted butter, cold and cubed
- 3/4 cup heavy cream

For the filling:

- 4 cups fresh strawberries, hulled and sliced
- 1/4 cup granulated sugar
- 1 cup heavy cream, whipped

Instructions:

1. Preheat the oven to 400°F (200°C). In a large bowl, combine flour, sugar, baking powder, and salt.
2. Add cold butter and cut it into the flour mixture using a pastry cutter or your fingers until it resembles coarse crumbs.
3. Pour in the heavy cream and stir until just combined.
4. Turn the dough out onto a floured surface, knead it a few times, and then roll it out to 1-inch thickness. Cut into rounds and place on a baking sheet.
5. Bake for 12-15 minutes, or until golden brown.
6. To assemble, slice the shortcakes in half and layer with strawberries and whipped cream. Serve immediately.

Raspberry Sorbet

Ingredients:

- 4 cups fresh raspberries
- 1 cup granulated sugar
- 1 cup water
- 2 tbsp lemon juice

Instructions:

1. In a saucepan, combine water and sugar. Heat over medium heat, stirring until the sugar has dissolved.
2. Add raspberries and lemon juice, and bring to a simmer for 5 minutes.
3. Puree the mixture in a blender or food processor, then strain through a fine mesh sieve to remove the seeds.
4. Cool the raspberry mixture completely, then transfer it to an ice cream maker and churn according to the manufacturer's instructions.
5. Freeze for at least 2 hours before serving.

Coconut Macaroons

Ingredients:

- 3 cups shredded sweetened coconut
- 1/2 cup granulated sugar
- 2 large egg whites
- 1 tsp vanilla extract
- 1/4 tsp salt
- 1/2 cup semisweet chocolate chips (optional)

Instructions:

1. Preheat the oven to 325°F (165°C) and line a baking sheet with parchment paper.
2. In a large bowl, combine coconut, sugar, egg whites, vanilla extract, and salt.
3. Scoop out tablespoon-sized portions of the coconut mixture and form into small mounds on the prepared baking sheet.
4. Bake for 20-25 minutes, or until golden brown. Let cool.
5. Optional: Melt the chocolate chips and drizzle over the cooled macaroons.

Carrot Cake with Cream Cheese Frosting

Ingredients:

For the cake:

- 2 cups all-purpose flour
- 1 1/2 tsp baking powder
- 1/2 tsp baking soda
- 1/2 tsp salt
- 1 1/2 tsp ground cinnamon
- 1/2 tsp ground nutmeg
- 1 cup vegetable oil
- 1 1/2 cups granulated sugar
- 4 large eggs
- 2 cups grated carrots
- 1 cup chopped walnuts (optional)

For the frosting:

- 8 oz cream cheese, softened
- 1/2 cup unsalted butter, softened
- 4 cups powdered sugar
- 1 tsp vanilla extract

Instructions:

1. Preheat the oven to 350°F (175°C). Grease and flour two 9-inch round cake pans.
2. In a bowl, whisk together flour, baking powder, baking soda, salt, cinnamon, and nutmeg.
3. In another bowl, whisk together oil, sugar, and eggs until smooth. Add the grated carrots and stir.
4. Gradually add the dry ingredients to the wet ingredients and mix until combined. Fold in walnuts if using.
5. Divide the batter evenly between the cake pans and bake for 30-35 minutes, or until a toothpick inserted comes out clean.
6. Let the cakes cool completely before frosting.
7. For the frosting, beat together cream cheese and butter until smooth. Gradually add powdered sugar and vanilla, mixing until fluffy.
8. Frost the cooled cakes and serve.

Profiteroles with Chocolate Sauce

Ingredients:

For the choux pastry:

- 1 cup water
- 1/2 cup unsalted butter
- 1 cup all-purpose flour
- 4 large eggs
- 1/4 tsp salt

For the filling:

- 1 1/2 cups heavy cream, whipped
- 1/4 cup powdered sugar

For the chocolate sauce:

- 1/2 cup heavy cream
- 4 oz semisweet chocolate, chopped
- 1 tbsp butter

Instructions:

1. Preheat the oven to 425°F (220°C). Line a baking sheet with parchment paper.
2. In a saucepan, bring water and butter to a boil. Remove from heat and stir in flour and salt. Return to the heat and cook, stirring constantly, until the mixture pulls away from the sides of the pan.
3. Remove from heat and let cool for 5 minutes. Add eggs one at a time, mixing until smooth after each addition.
4. Spoon or pipe the dough into small mounds on the baking sheet.
5. Bake for 20-25 minutes, or until puffed and golden.
6. Once the profiteroles are cool, slice them open and fill with whipped cream mixed with powdered sugar.
7. For the chocolate sauce, heat the cream in a saucepan until it simmers. Pour over the chopped chocolate and butter, stirring until smooth.
8. Drizzle the chocolate sauce over the filled profiteroles and serve.

Crème Brûlée

Ingredients:

- 2 cups heavy cream
- 1 vanilla bean, split and scraped (or 1 tbsp vanilla extract)
- 5 large egg yolks
- 1/2 cup granulated sugar
- 1/4 cup brown sugar (for topping)

Instructions:

1. Preheat the oven to 325°F (165°C). Place 4 ramekins in a baking dish.
2. In a saucepan, heat the cream and vanilla bean over medium heat until simmering. Remove from heat and let steep for 10 minutes.
3. Whisk the egg yolks and granulated sugar together in a bowl until pale and thick.
4. Gradually add the cream to the egg mixture, stirring constantly to prevent curdling.
5. Pour the mixture back into the saucepan and cook over low heat, stirring constantly, until it thickens enough to coat the back of a spoon.
6. Strain the mixture into a jug, then pour evenly into the ramekins.
7. Pour hot water into the baking dish, coming halfway up the sides of the ramekins. Bake for 45-50 minutes, or until set but still jiggly in the center.
8. Cool in the refrigerator for at least 4 hours.
9. Before serving, sprinkle brown sugar on top and caramelize with a kitchen torch.

Peach Cobbler

Ingredients:

For the filling:

- 4 cups fresh peaches, sliced
- 1/4 cup granulated sugar
- 1 tbsp cornstarch
- 1/4 tsp ground cinnamon
- 1 tbsp lemon juice

For the topping:

- 1 cup all-purpose flour
- 1/2 cup granulated sugar
- 1/4 tsp baking powder
- 1/4 tsp baking soda
- 1/4 tsp salt
- 1/2 cup unsalted butter, cold and cubed
- 1/4 cup milk

Instructions:

1. Preheat the oven to 375°F (190°C). In a bowl, combine peaches, sugar, cornstarch, cinnamon, and lemon juice. Transfer to a greased baking dish.
2. In a separate bowl, mix together flour, sugar, baking powder, baking soda, and salt. Cut in the cold butter until the mixture resembles coarse crumbs.
3. Add the milk and stir until combined. Drop spoonfuls of the topping over the peach filling.
4. Bake for 40-45 minutes, or until the topping is golden brown and the filling is bubbly.
5. Serve warm with vanilla ice cream or whipped cream.

Key Lime Pie

Ingredients:

- 1 1/2 cups graham cracker crumbs
- 1/4 cup granulated sugar
- 1/2 cup unsalted butter, melted
- 3 large egg yolks
- 1 can (14 oz) sweetened condensed milk
- 1/2 cup fresh lime juice
- 1 tbsp lime zest
- Whipped cream for topping

Instructions:

1. Preheat the oven to 350°F (175°C). In a bowl, combine graham cracker crumbs, sugar, and melted butter. Press into the bottom of a pie pan.
2. Bake the crust for 8-10 minutes, then let cool.
3. In a bowl, whisk together egg yolks, sweetened condensed milk, lime juice, and lime zest until smooth.
4. Pour the filling into the cooled crust and bake for 15-20 minutes, or until set.
5. Cool to room temperature, then refrigerate for at least 2 hours.
6. Top with whipped cream before serving.

Baklava

Ingredients:

- 1 package phyllo dough, thawed
- 2 cups mixed nuts (walnuts, pistachios, almonds), finely chopped
- 1 tsp ground cinnamon
- 1 1/2 cups unsalted butter, melted
- 1 cup granulated sugar
- 1 cup water
- 1/2 cup honey
- 1 tsp vanilla extract
- 1/2 tsp lemon juice

Instructions:

1. Preheat the oven to 350°F (175°C). Brush a 9x13-inch baking dish with melted butter.
2. Place a layer of phyllo dough in the dish and brush with butter. Repeat layering, brushing with butter between each sheet, until you have 8 layers.
3. In a bowl, combine the chopped nuts and cinnamon. Sprinkle a thin layer of the nut mixture over the phyllo dough.
4. Continue layering phyllo dough and butter, adding more nut mixture every 3-4 layers, until all nuts are used. Finish with 8 more layers of phyllo dough.
5. Cut the baklava into diamond or square shapes with a sharp knife.
6. Bake for 45-50 minutes, or until golden and crisp.
7. While baking, prepare the syrup by combining sugar, water, honey, vanilla extract, and lemon juice in a saucepan. Bring to a simmer and cook for 10 minutes.
8. Pour the hot syrup over the hot baklava once it's done baking. Let cool completely before serving.

Pavlova with Fresh Fruit

Ingredients:

For the meringue:

- 4 large egg whites
- 1 cup granulated sugar
- 1 tsp vanilla extract
- 1 tsp white vinegar
- 2 tsp cornstarch

For the topping:

- 1 cup heavy cream, whipped
- 1 tbsp powdered sugar
- 1 tsp vanilla extract
- Fresh fruit (kiwi, strawberries, blueberries, etc.)

Instructions:

1. Preheat the oven to 250°F (120°C). Line a baking sheet with parchment paper and draw a 9-inch circle on it.
2. In a clean bowl, beat the egg whites until soft peaks form. Gradually add sugar, one tablespoon at a time, until stiff peaks form.
3. Add vanilla extract, vinegar, and cornstarch. Beat until smooth and glossy.
4. Spoon the meringue mixture onto the prepared baking sheet, following the circle shape. Create a slight well in the center.
5. Bake for 1.5 hours, or until the meringue is crisp and dry to the touch. Turn off the oven and let the meringue cool completely.
6. Whip the heavy cream with powdered sugar and vanilla extract until stiff peaks form.
7. Once the meringue is cool, top with whipped cream and fresh fruit.
8. Serve immediately or refrigerate until ready to serve.

S'mores Bars

Ingredients:

- 1 1/2 cups graham cracker crumbs
- 1 cup all-purpose flour
- 1/2 cup unsweetened cocoa powder
- 1/2 tsp baking soda
- 1/4 tsp salt
- 1 cup unsalted butter, melted
- 1 cup packed brown sugar
- 2 large eggs
- 1 tsp vanilla extract
- 1 1/2 cups semisweet chocolate chips
- 2 cups mini marshmallows

Instructions:

1. Preheat the oven to 350°F (175°C). Line a 9x13-inch baking dish with parchment paper.
2. In a bowl, combine graham cracker crumbs, flour, cocoa powder, baking soda, and salt.
3. In another bowl, mix melted butter, brown sugar, eggs, and vanilla extract. Gradually stir in the dry ingredients.
4. Press the dough into the prepared baking dish. Sprinkle chocolate chips evenly over the dough.
5. Bake for 20-25 minutes, or until a toothpick inserted comes out clean.
6. Remove from the oven, and immediately sprinkle marshmallows on top. Return to the oven and bake for an additional 2-3 minutes, or until the marshmallows are golden.
7. Let cool completely before cutting into bars.

Churros with Cinnamon Sugar

Ingredients:

- 1 cup water
- 2 tbsp unsalted butter
- 1 tbsp granulated sugar
- 1/4 tsp salt
- 1 cup all-purpose flour
- 2 large eggs
- 1 tsp vanilla extract
- Vegetable oil for frying
- 1/2 cup granulated sugar (for coating)
- 1 tsp ground cinnamon (for coating)

Instructions:

1. In a saucepan, combine water, butter, sugar, and salt. Bring to a boil, then remove from heat and stir in the flour until smooth.
2. Let the dough cool for a few minutes, then add eggs one at a time, mixing well after each addition. Stir in vanilla extract.
3. Heat oil in a deep skillet or pan over medium heat to 375°F (190°C).
4. Transfer the dough to a piping bag fitted with a large star tip. Pipe strips of dough into the hot oil, cutting them to your desired length.
5. Fry the churros until golden brown, about 2-3 minutes per side.
6. Combine sugar and cinnamon in a bowl and coat the hot churros in the mixture.
7. Serve warm.

Blueberry Muffins

Ingredients:

- 2 cups all-purpose flour
- 1/2 cup granulated sugar
- 2 tsp baking powder
- 1/2 tsp baking soda
- 1/2 tsp salt
- 1/2 cup unsalted butter, melted
- 1 cup buttermilk
- 2 large eggs
- 1 tsp vanilla extract
- 1 1/2 cups fresh blueberries

Instructions:

1. Preheat the oven to 375°F (190°C). Line a muffin tin with paper liners.
2. In a large bowl, combine flour, sugar, baking powder, baking soda, and salt.
3. In another bowl, whisk together melted butter, buttermilk, eggs, and vanilla extract.
4. Gradually stir the wet ingredients into the dry ingredients until just combined. Gently fold in the blueberries.
5. Spoon the batter into the muffin cups, filling each about 2/3 full.
6. Bake for 20-25 minutes, or until a toothpick inserted comes out clean.
7. Let cool before serving.

Chocolate Eclairs

Ingredients:

For the choux pastry:

- 1 cup water
- 1/2 cup unsalted butter
- 1 cup all-purpose flour
- 4 large eggs
- 1/4 tsp salt

For the filling:

- 2 cups heavy cream
- 1/2 cup powdered sugar
- 1 tsp vanilla extract

For the chocolate glaze:

- 4 oz semisweet chocolate, chopped
- 1/4 cup heavy cream

Instructions:

1. Preheat the oven to 400°F (200°C). Line a baking sheet with parchment paper.
2. In a saucepan, bring water and butter to a boil. Stir in flour and salt, then cook over medium heat until the mixture forms a ball.
3. Remove from heat and let cool for 5 minutes. Add eggs one at a time, mixing well after each addition.
4. Pipe the dough onto the prepared baking sheet, forming long eclairs.
5. Bake for 20-25 minutes, or until golden and puffed. Let cool.
6. Whip the heavy cream, powdered sugar, and vanilla extract until stiff peaks form. Fill the eclairs with whipped cream.
7. For the glaze, heat heavy cream in a saucepan until simmering, then pour over the chopped chocolate. Stir until smooth.
8. Dip the filled eclairs into the chocolate glaze and let cool before serving.

Almond Joy Brownies

Ingredients:

For the brownies:

- 1 cup unsalted butter, melted
- 1 1/2 cups granulated sugar
- 4 large eggs
- 1 tsp vanilla extract
- 1 cup all-purpose flour
- 1/2 cup unsweetened cocoa powder
- 1/4 tsp salt
- 1/2 tsp baking powder

For the topping:

- 1 cup shredded coconut
- 1/2 cup whole almonds
- 1/2 cup semisweet chocolate chips

Instructions:

1. Preheat the oven to 350°F (175°C). Grease and flour a 9x13-inch baking dish.
2. In a bowl, combine melted butter, sugar, eggs, and vanilla extract. Mix until smooth.
3. In a separate bowl, whisk together flour, cocoa powder, salt, and baking powder. Gradually add the dry ingredients to the wet ingredients and mix until combined.
4. Pour the brownie batter into the prepared baking dish and smooth the top.
5. Sprinkle shredded coconut, almonds, and chocolate chips on top of the brownies.
6. Bake for 30-35 minutes, or until a toothpick inserted comes out clean.
7. Let cool before cutting into squares.

Classic Banana Pudding

Ingredients:

- 1 box vanilla wafers
- 4 ripe bananas, sliced
- 1 can (14 oz) sweetened condensed milk
- 2 cups cold milk
- 1 pkg (3.4 oz) instant vanilla pudding mix
- 1 cup heavy cream
- 1/4 cup powdered sugar
- 1 tsp vanilla extract

Instructions:

1. Line the bottom of a trifle dish or 9x13-inch dish with vanilla wafers.
2. Layer banana slices on top of the wafers.
3. In a bowl, whisk together sweetened condensed milk, cold milk, and pudding mix. Let it set for 5 minutes to thicken.
4. Spread the pudding mixture over the bananas and wafers.
5. In another bowl, whip the heavy cream with powdered sugar and vanilla extract until stiff peaks form. Spread the whipped cream over the pudding.
6. Garnish with additional vanilla wafers and banana slices.
7. Refrigerate for at least 2 hours before serving.

Fruit Tart with Pastry Cream

Ingredients:

For the tart crust:

- 1 1/4 cups all-purpose flour
- 1/4 cup powdered sugar
- 1/2 cup unsalted butter, cold and cubed
- 1 large egg yolk
- 1 tbsp ice water

For the pastry cream:

- 2 cups whole milk
- 1/2 cup granulated sugar
- 4 large egg yolks
- 1/4 cup cornstarch
- 1 tsp vanilla extract
- 2 tbsp unsalted butter

For the topping:

- Fresh seasonal fruit (berries, kiwi, citrus, etc.)
- Apricot jam (optional, for glazing)

Instructions:

1. Preheat the oven to 350°F (175°C). To make the crust, combine flour and powdered sugar in a bowl. Add the cubed butter and mix with a pastry cutter or your fingers until the mixture resembles breadcrumbs.
2. Add the egg yolk and ice water and mix until a dough forms. Wrap in plastic wrap and refrigerate for 30 minutes.
3. Roll out the dough on a floured surface and fit it into a tart pan. Prick the bottom with a fork and bake for 15-20 minutes, or until golden. Let it cool completely.
4. For the pastry cream, heat milk in a saucepan until warm. In a separate bowl, whisk together sugar, egg yolks, and cornstarch.
5. Gradually pour the warm milk into the egg mixture while whisking. Return the mixture to the saucepan and cook, whisking constantly, until it thickens. Remove from heat, stir in vanilla extract and butter, and let cool.
6. Once the tart shell has cooled, spread the pastry cream over the crust. Arrange the fresh fruit on top.
7. If desired, heat apricot jam and brush it over the fruit to give it a glossy finish. Serve chilled.

Sticky Toffee Pudding

Ingredients:

For the pudding:

- 1 1/2 cups pitted dates, chopped
- 1 tsp baking soda
- 1 1/2 cups boiling water
- 1/2 cup unsalted butter, softened
- 3/4 cup brown sugar
- 2 large eggs
- 1 1/2 cups all-purpose flour
- 1 tsp vanilla extract
- 1/2 tsp baking powder
- 1/4 tsp salt

For the toffee sauce:

- 1 cup heavy cream
- 1/2 cup brown sugar
- 1/4 cup unsalted butter
- 1 tsp vanilla extract

Instructions:

1. Preheat the oven to 350°F (175°C). Grease a baking dish or individual ramekins.
2. In a bowl, combine chopped dates and baking soda. Pour boiling water over the dates and set aside to soak for 10 minutes.
3. In a separate bowl, cream together butter and brown sugar. Add eggs one at a time and beat well.
4. Mix in flour, baking powder, salt, and vanilla extract. Add the soaked dates (along with the water) and stir until combined.
5. Pour the batter into the prepared baking dish and bake for 30-35 minutes, or until a toothpick inserted comes out clean.
6. While the pudding bakes, make the toffee sauce by combining heavy cream, brown sugar, butter, and vanilla extract in a saucepan. Bring to a simmer and cook for 5-7 minutes, or until it thickens slightly.
7. Once the pudding is done, pour half of the toffee sauce over the pudding. Serve warm with the remaining toffee sauce drizzled on top.

Lemon Bars

Ingredients:

For the crust:

- 1 1/2 cups all-purpose flour
- 1/2 cup powdered sugar
- 1/2 tsp salt
- 1/2 cup unsalted butter, cold and cubed

For the filling:

- 4 large eggs
- 1 1/2 cups granulated sugar
- 1/4 cup all-purpose flour
- 1/2 tsp baking powder
- 1/2 cup freshly squeezed lemon juice
- 1 tbsp lemon zest
- Powdered sugar for dusting

Instructions:

1. Preheat the oven to 350°F (175°C). Grease a 9x9-inch baking dish.
2. For the crust, combine flour, powdered sugar, and salt in a bowl. Cut in the cold butter until the mixture resembles coarse crumbs.
3. Press the dough into the bottom of the baking dish and bake for 15-20 minutes, or until lightly golden.
4. For the filling, whisk together eggs, granulated sugar, flour, baking powder, lemon juice, and lemon zest.
5. Pour the filling over the baked crust and return to the oven. Bake for an additional 20-25 minutes, or until set.
6. Let cool completely before cutting into squares. Dust with powdered sugar before serving.

Pistachio Gelato

Ingredients:

- 1 cup unsalted pistachios, shelled
- 1 1/2 cups whole milk
- 1/2 cup heavy cream
- 1/2 cup granulated sugar
- 4 large egg yolks
- 1 tsp vanilla extract
- A pinch of salt

Instructions:

1. In a food processor, pulse the pistachios until finely ground.
2. In a saucepan, heat milk, cream, and 1/4 cup of sugar over medium heat, stirring until the sugar dissolves.
3. In a bowl, whisk together egg yolks, remaining sugar, and ground pistachios until smooth.
4. Gradually pour the warm milk mixture into the egg mixture while whisking to temper the eggs. Return the mixture to the saucepan and cook over low heat, stirring constantly, until thickened (coats the back of a spoon).
5. Remove from heat, stir in vanilla extract and a pinch of salt. Let the mixture cool.
6. Chill the mixture in the refrigerator for at least 4 hours or overnight.
7. Once chilled, churn the mixture in an ice cream maker according to the manufacturer's instructions. Freeze until firm.

Chocolate Truffles

Ingredients:

- 8 oz semisweet or dark chocolate, chopped
- 1/2 cup heavy cream
- 1 tbsp unsalted butter
- 1 tsp vanilla extract
- Cocoa powder, chopped nuts, or melted chocolate for coating

Instructions:

1. Place the chopped chocolate in a heatproof bowl.
2. In a saucepan, heat the heavy cream and butter until it begins to simmer. Pour the hot cream over the chocolate and let it sit for 2-3 minutes.
3. Stir the mixture until smooth and glossy, then add vanilla extract.
4. Refrigerate the ganache for 1-2 hours, or until firm enough to scoop.
5. Use a melon baller or spoon to scoop out small portions of ganache and roll them into balls.
6. Coat the truffles in cocoa powder, chopped nuts, or melted chocolate.
7. Chill the truffles in the refrigerator until ready to serve.

Coconut Cream Pie

Ingredients:

For the crust:

- 1 1/2 cups graham cracker crumbs
- 1/4 cup granulated sugar
- 1/4 cup unsalted butter, melted

For the filling:

- 2 cups whole milk
- 1 can (14 oz) sweetened condensed milk
- 1/2 cup shredded coconut
- 3 large egg yolks
- 1/4 cup cornstarch
- 1/2 tsp vanilla extract
- 1/2 tsp coconut extract
- 1 cup heavy cream, whipped

Instructions:

1. Preheat the oven to 350°F (175°C). In a bowl, combine graham cracker crumbs, sugar, and melted butter. Press the mixture into the bottom of a pie pan to form the crust.
2. Bake for 10 minutes, then cool completely.
3. In a saucepan, combine whole milk, sweetened condensed milk, shredded coconut, and egg yolks. Bring to a simmer and whisk in cornstarch. Cook until thickened.
4. Stir in vanilla and coconut extract. Pour the filling into the cooled crust.
5. Refrigerate for at least 4 hours or until set.
6. Top with whipped cream and toasted coconut before serving.

Apple Fritters

Ingredients:

- 2 apples, peeled, cored, and chopped
- 1 1/2 cups all-purpose flour
- 1/4 cup sugar
- 1 tsp baking powder
- 1/2 tsp cinnamon
- 1/4 tsp salt
- 1/2 cup milk
- 2 large eggs
- 1 tsp vanilla extract
- Vegetable oil for frying
- Powdered sugar for dusting

Instructions:

1. In a bowl, combine flour, sugar, baking powder, cinnamon, and salt.
2. In a separate bowl, whisk together milk, eggs, and vanilla extract.
3. Add the wet ingredients to the dry ingredients and stir until combined. Fold in the chopped apples.
4. Heat oil in a deep skillet to 375°F (190°C).
5. Drop spoonfuls of batter into the hot oil and fry until golden brown, about 3-4 minutes per side.
6. Drain on paper towels and dust with powdered sugar before serving.

Baked Alaska

Ingredients:

For the cake layer:

- 1 store-bought or homemade sponge cake

For the ice cream:

- 4 cups of your favorite ice cream (vanilla, chocolate, etc.)

For the meringue:

- 4 large egg whites
- 1/2 cup granulated sugar
- 1/4 tsp cream of tartar

Instructions:

1. Preheat the oven to 500°F (260°C).
2. Slice the sponge cake to fit the base of a 9-inch round baking pan.
3. Soften the ice cream and spread it over the cake layer, smoothing it into an even layer. Freeze for 2 hours.
4. Beat egg whites with cream of tartar until soft peaks form. Gradually add sugar and continue to beat until stiff peaks form.
5. Remove the cake and ice cream from the freezer and cover with the meringue, sealing the edges.
6. Bake for 3-5 minutes, or until the meringue is golden brown.
7. Serve immediately.

Chocolate-Dipped Strawberries

Ingredients:

- 1 lb fresh strawberries, washed and dried
- 8 oz semisweet or dark chocolate, chopped
- 4 oz white chocolate, chopped (optional, for drizzling)

Instructions:

1. Line a baking sheet with parchment paper.
2. Melt the semisweet chocolate in a heatproof bowl over a pot of simmering water (double boiler method) or in the microwave in 30-second intervals, stirring between each.
3. Hold each strawberry by the stem and dip it into the melted chocolate, swirling to coat. Place the dipped strawberry on the prepared baking sheet.
4. If using white chocolate, melt it in the same manner and drizzle over the dipped strawberries.
5. Let the chocolate harden by placing the strawberries in the fridge for about 30 minutes before serving.

Cinnamon Rolls with Icing

Ingredients:

For the dough:

- 4 cups all-purpose flour
- 1/4 cup sugar
- 1 packet active dry yeast (2 1/4 tsp)
- 1 tsp salt
- 1 cup whole milk, warmed
- 1/4 cup unsalted butter, melted
- 2 large eggs

For the filling:

- 1/2 cup unsalted butter, softened
- 3/4 cup brown sugar, packed
- 2 tbsp ground cinnamon

For the icing:

- 1 cup powdered sugar
- 2 tbsp milk
- 1 tsp vanilla extract

Instructions:

1. In a large bowl, combine flour, sugar, yeast, and salt. Add the warm milk, melted butter, and eggs. Mix until a dough forms. Knead for about 5-7 minutes until smooth. Let rise in a warm place for 1-2 hours, or until doubled in size.
2. Preheat the oven to 350°F (175°C). Punch down the dough and roll it out on a floured surface into a 16x12-inch rectangle.
3. Spread softened butter over the dough, then sprinkle with brown sugar and cinnamon. Roll the dough tightly and cut into 12 even slices.
4. Place the rolls in a greased baking dish and let rise for another 30 minutes. Bake for 20-25 minutes, or until golden brown.
5. For the icing, whisk together powdered sugar, milk, and vanilla. Drizzle over the warm rolls before serving.

Molten Chocolate Mug Cake

Ingredients:

- 3 tbsp all-purpose flour
- 2 tbsp cocoa powder
- 3 tbsp granulated sugar
- 1/8 tsp baking powder
- 1/8 tsp salt
- 3 tbsp milk
- 2 tbsp vegetable oil
- 1/4 tsp vanilla extract
- 2 tbsp semisweet chocolate chips

Instructions:

1. In a microwave-safe mug, whisk together flour, cocoa powder, sugar, baking powder, and salt.
2. Add milk, oil, and vanilla extract to the dry ingredients and mix until smooth.
3. Stir in chocolate chips, then microwave on high for 1 minute and 20 seconds, or until the cake has risen and is set in the center.
4. Let cool for a minute before serving. Enjoy with a scoop of ice cream or a dollop of whipped cream.

Pear and Almond Galette

Ingredients:

For the crust:

- 1 1/2 cups all-purpose flour
- 1 tbsp sugar
- 1/2 tsp salt
- 1/2 cup unsalted butter, cold and cubed
- 3-4 tbsp ice water

For the filling:

- 3 ripe pears, peeled, cored, and sliced
- 1/4 cup almond meal
- 1/4 cup granulated sugar
- 1 tsp vanilla extract
- 1 tbsp lemon juice
- 1 tbsp butter, cut into small pieces
- 1 egg, beaten (for egg wash)

Instructions:

1. Preheat the oven to 375°F (190°C). In a bowl, combine flour, sugar, and salt. Cut in the butter until the mixture resembles coarse crumbs.
2. Gradually add ice water, stirring until the dough comes together. Wrap in plastic wrap and refrigerate for 30 minutes.
3. Roll out the dough on a floured surface into a 12-inch circle. Transfer to a parchment-lined baking sheet.
4. For the filling, toss the pear slices with almond meal, sugar, vanilla extract, and lemon juice. Arrange the pear slices in the center of the dough, leaving a border.
5. Fold the edges of the dough over the filling. Dot with butter and brush the crust with beaten egg.
6. Bake for 35-40 minutes, or until the crust is golden brown. Let cool before serving.

Salted Caramel Flan

Ingredients:

For the caramel:

- 1/2 cup granulated sugar
- 2 tbsp water

For the flan:

- 1 can (14 oz) sweetened condensed milk
- 1 can (12 oz) evaporated milk
- 3 large eggs
- 1 tbsp vanilla extract
- 1/4 tsp salt

Instructions:

1. Preheat the oven to 350°F (175°C). In a small saucepan, combine sugar and water over medium heat. Stir until the sugar dissolves, then let it cook for about 5 minutes, until amber in color.
2. Immediately pour the caramel into the bottom of individual ramekins or a flan dish, swirling to coat the bottoms. Set aside to cool.
3. For the flan, whisk together sweetened condensed milk, evaporated milk, eggs, vanilla, and salt. Pour the mixture over the caramel in the ramekins.
4. Place the ramekins in a baking dish and pour hot water into the dish to create a water bath. Bake for 45-50 minutes, or until set (a knife inserted should come out clean).
5. Cool completely before refrigerating for at least 2 hours. To serve, run a knife around the edges and invert onto a plate.

Tarte Tatin

Ingredients:

- 6-8 medium apples (preferably Granny Smith or Golden Delicious)
- 1/2 cup unsalted butter
- 1 cup granulated sugar
- 1 tsp vanilla extract
- 1 sheet puff pastry, thawed
- Whipped cream (optional)

Instructions:

1. Preheat the oven to 375°F (190°C). Peel, core, and halve the apples.
2. In a 9-inch ovenproof skillet, melt butter over medium heat. Add sugar and cook until it begins to turn golden brown.
3. Add the apples to the skillet, arranging them tightly in a spiral pattern. Cook for 15-20 minutes, until the apples are tender and caramelized.
4. Remove the pan from heat and add vanilla extract.
5. Roll out the puff pastry and drape it over the apples, tucking the edges into the pan.
6. Bake for 25-30 minutes, or until the pastry is golden. Let cool for a few minutes, then carefully invert onto a serving plate.
7. Serve warm with whipped cream, if desired.

Pumpkin Pie

Ingredients:

For the crust:

- 1 1/4 cups all-purpose flour
- 1/4 tsp salt
- 1/2 cup unsalted butter, cold and cubed
- 3-4 tbsp ice water

For the filling:

- 2 cups canned pumpkin puree
- 3/4 cup brown sugar
- 2 tsp ground cinnamon
- 1/2 tsp ground ginger
- 1/4 tsp ground nutmeg
- 1/4 tsp ground cloves
- 1/2 tsp salt
- 3 large eggs
- 1 1/2 cups heavy cream
- 1 tsp vanilla extract

Instructions:

1. Preheat the oven to 375°F (190°C). For the crust, combine flour and salt in a bowl. Cut in butter until the mixture resembles coarse crumbs.
2. Gradually add ice water, mixing until the dough comes together. Roll out and fit into a pie dish. Refrigerate while preparing the filling.
3. In a large bowl, whisk together pumpkin puree, sugar, spices, and salt. Add eggs, cream, and vanilla, whisking until smooth.
4. Pour the filling into the prepared crust and bake for 45-50 minutes, or until the center is set.
5. Let cool before serving. Serve with whipped cream if desired.

Chocolate Pots de Crème

Ingredients:

- 8 oz semisweet or dark chocolate, chopped
- 1 1/2 cups heavy cream
- 1/2 cup whole milk
- 4 large egg yolks
- 1/4 cup granulated sugar
- 1 tsp vanilla extract

Instructions:

1. Preheat the oven to 325°F (160°C). Place chocolate in a heatproof bowl.
2. In a saucepan, heat cream and milk over medium heat until simmering. Pour over the chocolate and stir until melted.
3. In a bowl, whisk egg yolks and sugar. Slowly add the chocolate mixture, whisking constantly.
4. Strain the mixture through a fine-mesh sieve and pour into ramekins.
5. Place the ramekins in a baking dish and fill the dish with hot water to create a water bath. Bake for 25-30 minutes, or until the custard is set.
6. Chill for at least 2 hours before serving.

Butterscotch Pudding

Ingredients:

- 1/2 cup unsalted butter
- 1 cup brown sugar, packed
- 2 cups whole milk
- 1/4 tsp salt
- 2 tsp vanilla extract
- 2 large egg yolks
- 3 tbsp cornstarch

Instructions:

1. In a saucepan, melt butter and brown sugar over medium heat until smooth. Add milk and salt, bringing to a simmer.
2. In a separate bowl, whisk egg yolks and cornstarch. Gradually pour in some of the hot milk mixture to temper the yolks.
3. Pour the egg mixture back into the saucepan, whisking constantly until thickened.
4. Remove from heat and stir in vanilla extract. Pour into bowls and chill for at least 2 hours before serving.

Orange Sorbet

Ingredients:

- 2 cups fresh orange juice
- 1 cup water
- 1/2 cup granulated sugar
- 1 tbsp lemon juice (optional, for added tartness)

Instructions:

1. In a saucepan, combine the water and sugar. Heat over medium heat, stirring occasionally until the sugar dissolves.
2. Remove from heat and let the syrup cool completely.
3. Stir in the fresh orange juice and lemon juice (if using).
4. Pour the mixture into an ice cream maker and churn according to the manufacturer's instructions.
5. Transfer to an airtight container and freeze for 2-3 hours before serving.

Snickerdoodle Cookies

Ingredients:

- 2 3/4 cups all-purpose flour
- 2 tsp cream of tartar
- 1 tsp baking soda
- 1/4 tsp salt
- 1 cup unsalted butter, softened
- 1 1/2 cups granulated sugar
- 2 large eggs
- 1 tsp vanilla extract
- 2 tbsp granulated sugar
- 2 tsp ground cinnamon

Instructions:

1. Preheat the oven to 350°F (175°C). Line baking sheets with parchment paper.
2. In a bowl, whisk together flour, cream of tartar, baking soda, and salt.
3. In a separate large bowl, beat the butter and sugar until creamy. Add eggs and vanilla, and mix until smooth.
4. Gradually add the dry ingredients, mixing until just combined.
5. In a small bowl, combine the cinnamon and sugar. Roll the dough into 1-inch balls and roll each ball in the cinnamon-sugar mixture.
6. Place the cookies on the prepared baking sheets, spaced about 2 inches apart. Bake for 8-10 minutes, or until lightly golden. Let cool on a wire rack.

Chocolate-Covered Pretzels

Ingredients:

- 1 cup semisweet or milk chocolate chips
- 1 cup white chocolate chips (optional, for drizzling)
- 2 cups mini pretzels
- Sprinkles (optional)

Instructions:

1. Melt the semisweet chocolate chips in a microwave-safe bowl in 30-second intervals, stirring in between until smooth.
2. Dip each pretzel into the melted chocolate, using a fork to coat it fully. Place on a parchment-lined baking sheet.
3. If using white chocolate, melt it the same way and drizzle over the chocolate-covered pretzels.
4. Add sprinkles if desired and let the pretzels cool at room temperature, or place them in the fridge to speed up the process.

Mousse au Chocolat

Ingredients:

- 8 oz semisweet or dark chocolate, chopped
- 3/4 cup heavy cream
- 3 large eggs, separated
- 1/4 cup granulated sugar
- 1 tsp vanilla extract

Instructions:

1. Melt the chocolate in a heatproof bowl over a pot of simmering water (double boiler method), stirring until smooth. Let cool slightly.
2. Whip the heavy cream until stiff peaks form. Set aside.
3. In a separate bowl, beat the egg yolks with sugar and vanilla until pale and thick.
4. Gradually fold the melted chocolate into the egg yolk mixture.
5. In another bowl, beat the egg whites until stiff peaks form. Gently fold the egg whites into the chocolate mixture.
6. Finally, fold in the whipped cream until well combined.
7. Spoon the mousse into serving dishes and chill for at least 2 hours before serving.

Fruit and Cream Parfaits

Ingredients:

- 1 1/2 cups mixed fresh fruit (berries, kiwi, mango, etc.)
- 2 cups heavy cream
- 2 tbsp powdered sugar
- 1 tsp vanilla extract
- 1/2 cup granola (optional)

Instructions:

1. Whip the heavy cream with powdered sugar and vanilla extract until soft peaks form.
2. In serving glasses, layer the whipped cream, fresh fruit, and granola (if using).
3. Repeat the layers until the glasses are filled, finishing with a layer of whipped cream.
4. Garnish with additional fresh fruit or a drizzle of honey.
5. Chill for 30 minutes before serving.

Ricotta Cheesecake

Ingredients:

For the crust:

- 1 1/2 cups graham cracker crumbs
- 1/4 cup sugar
- 1/2 cup unsalted butter, melted

For the filling:

- 2 lbs ricotta cheese, drained
- 1 cup granulated sugar
- 3 large eggs
- 1 tsp vanilla extract
- 1 tbsp lemon zest
- 1/4 cup all-purpose flour

Instructions:

1. Preheat the oven to 350°F (175°C). Grease a 9-inch springform pan.
2. In a bowl, combine graham cracker crumbs, sugar, and melted butter. Press into the bottom of the prepared pan to form the crust.
3. In a separate bowl, mix ricotta cheese, sugar, eggs, vanilla, and lemon zest. Gradually add the flour and mix until smooth.
4. Pour the filling into the prepared crust and bake for 45-50 minutes, or until the cheesecake is set and lightly golden on top.
5. Let cool to room temperature, then refrigerate for at least 4 hours before serving.

Almond Cake with Apricot Glaze

Ingredients:

For the cake:

- 1 cup almond meal
- 1/2 cup all-purpose flour
- 1 tsp baking powder
- 1/4 tsp salt
- 1/2 cup unsalted butter, softened
- 1 cup granulated sugar
- 3 large eggs
- 1 tsp vanilla extract
- 1/4 cup milk

For the glaze:

- 1/2 cup apricot preserves
- 1 tbsp water

Instructions:

1. Preheat the oven to 350°F (175°C). Grease and flour a 9-inch round cake pan.
2. In a bowl, combine almond meal, flour, baking powder, and salt.
3. In a separate bowl, beat the butter and sugar until light and fluffy. Add the eggs one at a time, beating well after each addition.
4. Add vanilla extract and milk, then fold in the dry ingredients.
5. Pour the batter into the prepared pan and bake for 30-35 minutes, or until a toothpick inserted into the center comes out clean.
6. For the glaze, heat apricot preserves and water in a saucepan until smooth. Brush over the warm cake.
7. Let the cake cool before serving.

Lavender Honey Ice Cream

Ingredients:

- 2 cups heavy cream
- 1 cup whole milk
- 3/4 cup honey
- 1 tbsp dried lavender buds
- 5 large egg yolks
- 1 tsp vanilla extract

Instructions:

1. In a saucepan, heat the cream, milk, honey, and lavender over medium heat until just simmering. Remove from heat and let steep for 15 minutes.
2. Strain out the lavender buds and return the mixture to the saucepan.
3. Whisk the egg yolks in a separate bowl. Slowly pour the warm cream mixture into the yolks while whisking constantly.
4. Return the mixture to the saucepan and cook over low heat, stirring constantly, until it thickens and coats the back of a spoon.
5. Remove from heat and stir in vanilla extract. Let the mixture cool, then chill in the refrigerator for at least 4 hours.
6. Churn in an ice cream maker according to the manufacturer's instructions, then freeze for 2-3 hours before serving.

Zucchini Bread with Walnuts

Ingredients:

- 2 cups all-purpose flour
- 1 tsp baking soda
- 1/2 tsp salt
- 1 tsp ground cinnamon
- 1/2 tsp ground nutmeg
- 1 cup granulated sugar
- 1/2 cup vegetable oil
- 2 large eggs
- 2 cups grated zucchini (about 2 medium zucchinis)
- 1/2 cup chopped walnuts

Instructions:

1. Preheat the oven to 350°F (175°C). Grease a 9x5-inch loaf pan.
2. In a bowl, whisk together flour, baking soda, salt, cinnamon, and nutmeg.
3. In a separate bowl, mix sugar and oil until well combined. Add eggs one at a time, mixing well after each.
4. Stir in grated zucchini, then gradually add the dry ingredients and mix until just combined. Fold in walnuts.
5. Pour the batter into the prepared pan and bake for 50-60 minutes, or until a toothpick inserted into the center comes out clean.
6. Let cool in the pan for 10 minutes before transferring to a wire rack to cool completely.

www.ingramcontent.com/pod-product-compliance
Lightning Source LLC
LaVergne TN
LVHW081330060526
838201LV00055B/2555